THE SAVVY ENTREPRENEUR

The Ultimate Guide To Entrepreneurial Success: Mindset, Strategies, and Beyond

Disclaimer

This eBook has been written for information purposes only. Every effort has been made to make this eBook as complete and accurate as possible. However, there may be mistakes in typography or content. Also, this eBook provides information only up to the publishing date. Therefore, this eBook should be used as a guide - not as the ultimate source.

The purpose of this eBook is to educate. The author and the publisher do not warrant that the information contained in this eBook is fully complete and shall not be responsible for any errors or omissions. The author and publisher shall have neither liability nor responsibility to any person or entity with respect to any loss or damage caused or alleged to be caused directly or indirectly by this ebook.

This eBook offers information and is designed for educational purposes only. You should not rely on this information as a substitute, nor does it replace professional medical advice, diagnosis, or treatment.

Table of Contents

Introduction

Introduction

You've decided to enter into the fast-paced and ever-evolving world of business, an exhilarating and challenging endeavor. The journey of building and growing a successful business requires more than simply a good idea and hard work. It demands a unique mindset and effective strategies that can withstand the trials and tribulations that come with entrepreneurship.

Mindset and strategies serve as the twin pillars upon which entrepreneurial success is built. They are the driving forces that ignite that spark of innovation, fuel determination, and enable entrepreneurs, like yourself, to navigate the complex and ever-changing business landscape.

Whether you're a seasoned businessperson looking to enhance your skills or a budding visionary embarking on your new voyage, understanding and harnessing the power of mindset and how to create winning strategies will significantly influence your chances of success.

Why does mindset matter? The mindset of an entrepreneur shapes their perspective, decision-making, and resilience in the face of challenges. It is the foundation upon which you build your businesses, fostering creativity, adaptability, and a relentless pursuit of your goals.

For instance, a growth mindset propels entrepreneurs to view obstacles as opportunities for learning and development, enabling them to bounce back from failures and setbacks with renewed determination.

On the same token, your strategies form the blueprint for your success. A well-crafted strategy acts as a roadmap and guide towards your main objectives, allocating resources effectively, and capitalizing on opportunities. A good strategy ensures that every action taken aligns with the overall vision, fostering a sense of direction and purpose. Practicing effective strategies allows you to leverage all your strengths, mitigate risks, and optimize your chances of achieving sustainable growth in your business.

Success as an entrepreneur is not determined by luck or circumstances; it's a result of deliberate choices, a good mindset, and well-executed strategies. But how do entrepreneurs acquire these skills? Let's take a look.

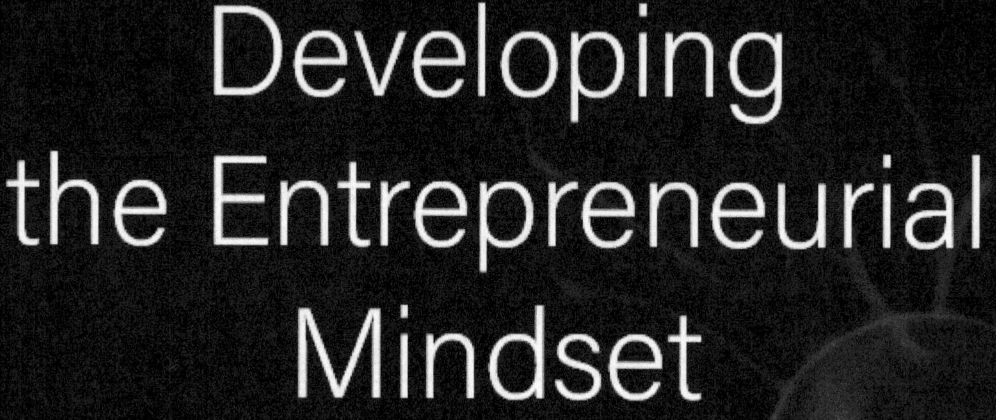
Developing
the Entrepreneurial
Mindset

Chapter 1: Developing the Entrepreneurial Mindset

It's not just about having a brilliant idea or a unique product, but that's a great start. You have to cultivate the right mindset—a way of thinking and approaching challenges that sets you apart from the rest.

There are a number of traits and characteristics that successful entrepreneurs possess, and you can develop yourself to enhance your chances of achieving your goals.

Understanding the traits and characteristics of successful entrepreneurs

1. Passion and Vision: The key driving for behind entrepreneurs is passion. Successful entrepreneurs possess a deep-seated enthusiasm for their ideas, products, or services, that fuels their determination and commitment. A clear vision guides that drive down the right path, helping them set ambitious goals and navigate over the obstacles with incredible focus.

2. Resilience and Perseverance: This type of life path is not for the faint of heart. It requires considerable resilience in the face of adversity and the ability to persevere through many challenges and failures. Successful entrepreneurs understand that setbacks are merely

stepping stone to success. They embrace failures as opportunities to learn and grow, bouncing back with renewed determination and adaptability.

3. Risk-Taking and Decision-Making: Entrepreneurs are comfortable taking risks. Not any risks, but calculated risks. They understand that sometimes extraordinary results require them to take a step outside of their comfort zone and embrace uncertainty. Successful entrepreneurs possess a keen sense of judgment and the ability to make quick and informed decisions, weighing the potential rewards against the risks involved.

4. Innovative Thinking: At the core of entrepreneurship lies innovation. Successful entrepreneurs possess a knack for thinking outside of the box, challenging the status quo, and identifying new opportunities. They constantly seek ways to improve existing products or services, disrupt industries, and meet unmet needs in the market.

5. Adaptability and Flexibility: The world of business is constantly evolving, and successful entrepreneurs adapt and evolve with it. They are quick to respond to changes, whether it's market trends, customer preferences, or technologies. Those that embrace change and adjust their strategies accordingly are better positioned to thrive in these dynamic environments.

6. Continuous Learning: Successful entrepreneurs are lifelong learners. They possess a curiosity to explore new ideas, acquire new skills, and stay ahead of the curve. They invest heavily in their personal and professional development, seeking knowledge through books, mentors,

networking events, and industry conferences. By constantly expanding their knowledge base, they gain a competitive edge and stay at the forefront of their industries.

7. Self-Confidence and Self-Belief: Believing in yourself is crucial for success. You need a strong sense of self-confidence, which allows you to take risks, pitch your ideas, and persevere through challenges. Successful entrepreneurs trust their instincts and have faith in their abilities, even when faced with skepticism or criticism.

While some are born and raised with these traits and characteristics, they can be learned too. You can cultivate the mindset necessary to overcome obstacles, embrace innovation, and seize opportunities.

How to develop a growth mindset and overcome limiting beliefs

Remember, your mindset shapes your actions and outcomes. By fostering a growth mindset, or the idea that abilities and intelligence can be developed through dedication and hard work, you can continuously develop the skills and abilities necessary for entrepreneurial success.

To shift your fixed mindset to a growth mindset, add the word "yet" to your vocabulary. When faced with a challenge or setback, remind yourself that you haven't achieved success "yet". This simple shift in language opens up possibilities and reinforces the belief that you have the capacity to learn and grow.

It's easy enough to embrace the idea that you need to cultivate your personal and professional development. You'll want to embrace that concept that you should be always learning and growing. View every experience, whether it's a success or failure, as an opportunity for growth and learning. Seek out new knowledge, read books, attend workshops, and engage in continuous self-improvement. There's always room for new ideas and new paths.

A growth mindset requires you to change your perspective of failure. Rather than seeing it as a reflection of your abilities, view it as a valuable learning experience. Analyze your failures, extract lessons from them, and apply those lessons to future endeavors. Try to understand that failure is an inevitable part of your entrepreneurial journey and an opportunity for you to grow and improve.

Learning to identify the beliefs you hold that limit you is a large part of opening up that growth mindset. Limiting beliefs hold you back and are often based on past experiences or societal conditioning. Fight these beliefs by replacing negative self-talk with positive affirmations and reframe your mindset to focus on possibilities rather than limitations.

Using the peers around you can help keep your mindset in check and aim for growth. Inviting feedback from mentors, peers, and customers is an opportunity to improve. Constructive criticism doesn't have to be damaging. Work on developing the ability to separate your self-worth from feedback. It helps to surround yourself with a growth-minded community who have the same goals as you're striving for.

Strategies for maintaining motivation and resilience

One of the greatest obstacles you will face is maintaining your motivation and resilience. Building and growing a business can be challenging and unpredictable, requiring strategies to sustain your drive and bounce back from setbacks.

One key strategy is setting clear goals and creating a vision. Clearly define what you want to achieve and break down goals into actionable steps, providing direction and purpose. Understanding your "why" behind your entrepreneurial endeavors is another important aspect, as it connects you to your deeper motivations and helps you stay committed during difficult times.

Celebrating small wins along the way boost motivation and reinforces that positive mindset. Taking care of your physical and mental well-being through self-care activities such as exercise, proper nutrition, and relaxation is essential. Building a support network of mentors and like-minded individuals provides guidance, inspiration, and encouragement.

Remember, maintaining motivation and resilience and that growth mindset is an ongoing process that requires consistent effort and self-care.

Mastering the Art of Decision Making

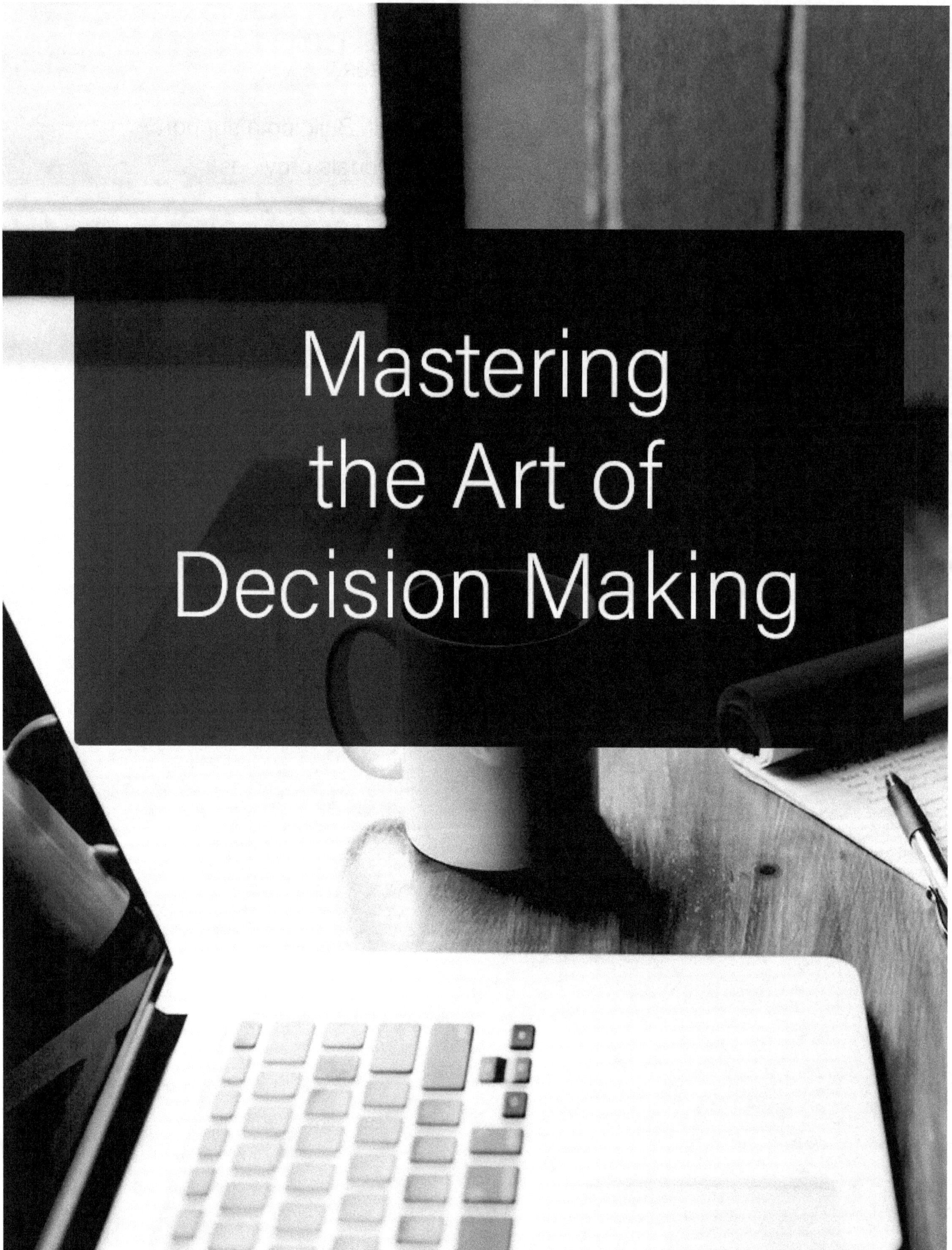

Chapter 2: Mastering the Art of Decision Making

Making decisions with limited information and uncertain outcomes

Decision-making is a skill that you must master. It becomes particularly challenging when decisions need to be made with limited information and in the face of uncertain outcomes. The ability to navigate these situations and make effective decisions is crucial to the success of any business.

Before making any decision, clearly define the criteria that will guide your evaluation. Identify the key factors that are most important to you and your business. This helps you focus on what truly matters and provides a framework for weighing out options, even when information is limited.

Even is information is scarce, it's important to gather as much relevant data as possible. Tap into your network, conduct research, and seek expert opinions, if they exist, to gain insights and perspectives. Look for patterns and trends that can inform your decision, even if you don't have complete information.

With the information at hand, consider the potential risks and uncertainties associated with each decision. Identify the worst-case scenarios and develop contingency plans to mitigate the risks. The proactive approach allows you to address potential challenges and provides a sense of preparedness, even in uncertain situations.

In situations where information is limited, sometimes it's best to embrace the test-and-learn approach. Make small, low-risk experiments or prototypes to gather some real-time feedback and validate your assumptions. This process enables you to learn from outcomes and make for informed decisions over time.

Eventually, as you grow, intuition will play a deeper role in your decision making. While data and analysis are important, it's your intuition that often guides you through these dynamic environments when quick decisions are necessary. Trust in your instincts that got you where you are, draw upon your experience and expertise, and combine it with the available information to make the best possible decision.

Understanding risk and reward

The decisions you'll be required to make involve a delicate balance between risk and reward. Entrepreneurs must assess the potential risks and weigh them against the potential rewards of a particular action. Understanding the dynamics of this relationship is crucial for making informed decisions.

To make sound decisions, you'll need to understand the risk and reward within your business context. Risk refers to the possibility of negative outcomes or losses, while reward represents potential benefits and gains. Defining these terms for your business allows for more effective decision making.

For each decision you'll want to identify and evaluate potential risks associated with that choice. Consider both internal and external factors and quantify risks by assigning probabilities and potential impacts. The process will help you understand the magnitude of the risks involved.

Next, analyze and quantify potential rewards tied to the decision. Consider financial gains, market opportunities, competitive advantages, and other positive outcomes. Understanding potential rewards aids in evaluating the upside of a decision.

Each entrepreneur will have a different risk tolerance. You'll need to gauge and understand your comfort level with taking risks and the potential impact on your business and personal life. Consider factors like financial stability, industry dynamics, and personal goals to align your decisions with your "risk appetite".

Risk management strategies are also a good idea. Performing tasks like scenario analysis to explore the various outcomes based on different levels of risk and reward can help mitigate identified risks and minimize the potential negative impacts. Proactive risk management strengthens your decision making and helps you to navigate uncertainties. Sometimes, it's hard to make a decision when you need to.

Overcoming decision paralysis and analysis paralysis

Decisions can be hard to make even with plenty of information at your fingertips. Situations will occur where you become overwhelmed by the abundance of choices or get trapped in an endless cycle of overthinking and analyzing. Overcoming these obstacles is critical for maintaining progress and making timely decision, but how?

To avoid decision paralysis, establish clear criteria for making decisions. Identify the key factors that are most relevant to your situation and prioritize them. As we mentioned before, break it down into manageable pieces. Having a set of predefined criteria narrows down the options you have to consider and facilitates a more focuses process.

Deadlines create a sense of urgency and anxiety but establishing a realistic timeline in which you'll make decisions can prevent unnecessary delays. Breaking down complex decisions into smaller steps and assigning timeframes to each step helps to overcome any analysis paralysis.

We're often faced with numerous choices and it's essential to streamline and limit these options. To overcome paralysis, identify a small number of alternatives that align with your criteria and eliminate unnecessary choices. By reducing the number of options, you can concentrate on a more manageable selection.

Decision making is a skill that can be developed through practice and self-awareness. By breaking down your decisions into more manageable pieces and processes you can learn from your past and grow your natural instincts and break free from paralysis, making more effective choices.

Navigating Failure and Success

Chapter 3: Navigating Failure and Success

On your entrepreneurial journey, both failure and success are inevitable. How you navigate failure and leverage it as a stepping stone to success plays a crucial role in your growth and resilience. Failure can be a valuable teacher, providing lessons and insights that fuel your future success.

Learning from failure and using it to fuel success

By adopting that growth mindset, you can begin to see failure as an opportunity for learning and growth. Instead of viewing failure as a reflection of your abilities, consider it as a temporary setback and an invitation to improve. Embrace challenges and setbacks as learning experiences that build that resilience and fuel that drive you have toward success.

It helps to take the time to reflect on your failures and analyze the factors that led to them. Identify the specific mistakes, weaknesses, or gaps in your approach. Extract valuable lessons from each failure and use them as insights for your future decisions.

Don't take failure as a personal defeat, but rather simply feedback. Understand that any failures provide you with valuable information about what doesn't work, allowing you to refine your approach and your strategies. By reframing failure as feedback, you can detach yourself emotionally and then objectively analyze the situation.

After collecting all this knowledge, use it. Iterate and pivot your strategies. Make adjustments, experiment with new approaches, and adapt to changing circumstances. Embrace a flexible mindset that welcomes change and sees it as an opportunity for that growth and then success.

Amidst failures it's important to celebrate the small wins along the way. Recognize the progress you make, no matter how small, as it reinforces a positive mindset and provides that needed motivation and therefore resilience.

Failure is not an endpoint but a stepping stone on the road to achievement.

Handling success and avoiding complacency

Success is an exhilarating milestone, but also present its own unique challenges. Handling success effectively requires maintaining momentum, avoiding complacency, and continuously striving for growth.

Even in the face of success, maintain that growth mindset. You need to view success as a stepping stone as well rather than a destination. Recognize that there is always room for improvement and that continued growth and learning are essential to sustain your success.

To avoid settling into that complacency that often comes with great success, set some ambitious goals. These are goals that push you outside of that comfort zone. Challenge yourself to achieve new milestones and strive for excellence. Setting specific, measurable, and time-bound goals keep you focused and motivated.

Within your business, it helps to cultivate a culture of continuous improvement. Encourage any employees to seek out opportunities for innovation and optimization. Use both internal and external feedback to identify areas for growth.

Because complacency often stems from stagnation, it's good to seek out new challenges that stretch your capabilities and expand your horizons. This can come from exploring new markets, developing new products or services, or taking on projects that push the boundaries of your personal expertise.

It's perfectly fine to celebrate your successes, and you should, but remain grounded. Avoid letting success inflate your ego or blind you to potential pitfalls. Stay humble, maintain your perspective, and remember the hard work and dedication that contributed to your newfound success.

Developing a healthy relationship with both failure and success

Developing a healthy relationship with both these things, failure and success, is essential for long-term growth and well-being.

By shifting your perspective on failure and viewing it as a valuable learning experience you recognize that failure is a natural part of the process and an opportunity for growth. Be kind to yourself when faced with failure. Avoid self-blame and self-criticism, as these negative emotions can hinder your ability to bounce back. Practicing self-compassion with understanding, forgiveness, and encouragement goes a long way.

Learn from your failures so you can better celebrate your success. When experiencing success, practice gratitude and acknowledge the efforts that contributed to that success. Celebrate your milestones both big and small and express gratitude towards your team, mentors, and supporters who played a role in your success. The gratitude is important to maintain that growth mindset and maintain humility.

Remaining humble is a much healthier relationship to establish with success. Recognize that success is often the result of a collective effort and external factors beyond your control. Avoid excessive pride or arrogance, as it can hinder personal growth and strain relationships.

Both success and failure should be viewed as opportunities for continuous growth. Strive to constantly improve yourself, your business, and your skills. Set new goals, challenge yourself, and seek out new opportunities for learning and development. Embrace that mindset of lifelong learning and adaptability.

Maintaining a balance perspective on both failure and success is optimal. Remember that failure does not define your worth, and success does not guarantee eternal triumph. Stay grounded, maintain perspective, and recognize that the entrepreneurial journey is a series of ups and downs. Cultivate resilience and the ability to adapt to changing circumstances.

Idea Generation and Validation

Chapter 4: Idea Generation and Validation

The foundation of any successful business is a great idea. But how do entrepreneurs generate and validate ideas that are both innovative and viable?

Finding and validating business ideas

The first step in generating a business idea is to identify a problem that needs to be solved. Look for pain points, unmet needs, and inefficiencies in the market or in your own experiences. Brainstorm solutions that can address these problems and create value for potential customers.

Once you've identified a problem and potential solutions, research the market to determine if there is a demand for your idea. Analyze the competition, target audience, and industry trends to assess the feasibility of your idea. Use this information to refine your concept and determine if there is a market fit.

Always validate and idea before investing significant time and resources into it. You'll want to gather feedback from potential customers, industry experts, and mentors to refine your concept and identify the potential roadblocks. Test your idea through prototypes, minimum viable products, and pilot programs to assess its viability and make any adjustments to your strategy.

There's also financial viability to consider. A great idea also needs to be financially viable, Assess the costs associated with launching and running your business, including production, marketing, and operational expenses. Determine what your revenue streams are and projected profits to ensure that your idea can sustain a profitable business model.

In order to stand out in a crowded market, your business idea must have a unique value proposition that differentiates it apart from the competition. Determine what sets your idea apart, whether it is a unique feature, competitive pricing, or superior customer service.

Understanding market demand and competition

It's essential that you target the right audience and develop effective strategies when it comes to market demand and competition.

Conducting marketing research is the first step in understanding your potential market demand and what competition is waiting for you. Research gives you insights into customer needs, preferences, and behaviors. Analyze demographic data, conduct surveys and interviews, and utilize focus groups to gather information about your target audience. You need to understand their pain points, desires, and buying habits to tailor your offerings to their specific needs.

You're going to want to study your competitors. You need to understand their strengths and weaknesses and their current position in the market. Study their product offerings, pricing, marketing strategies, and customer reviews. This research helps you find gaps in the market and differentiate your offerings from your competitors.

Based on all of this collected information, narrow down your target market. You want to define your ideal customer profile and create buyer personas to understand their characteristics and preferences. This will help you later on when you start on marketing strategies, but now helps develop products that will align with their needs.

Now that you have your target market you can assess its growth potential. Determine if this market is large enough to support your proposed business. Will there be opportunities for expansion? Consider factors like market trends, economic conditions, and industry forecasts to gauge the market's future viability.

Market demand and competition are dynamic. Continuously monitor market trends, customer feedback, and competitor strategies. Stay updated on industry developments, emerging technologies, and changing customer preferences. Then you can adapt your offerings and strategies accordingly to stay competitive and meet evolving market demands.

Developing and testing a Minimum Viable Product (MVP)

It's been mentioned briefly already. But the concept of a Minimum Viable Product (MVP) has become a popular approach for entrepreneurs to test and validate their business ideas in a cost-effective and efficient manner.

To develop an MVP for your business you'll first need to identify the core value or key features that your product or service will offer to solve the target market's problem. Determine the essential functionality that delivers the most significant value to users. This helps in prioritizing development efforts and keeping the MVP focused.

With this core value in place, develop a basic prototype or a simplified version of your product or service that demonstrates this value. The prototype can be a mock-up, wireframe, or a basic functional version that showcases those key features you decided on. The goal is to provide a tangible representation of your idea that can be tested and therefore validated.

Find a select group of early adopters of target customers who are willing to provide feedback. You're going to share the MVP with them and observe their interactions and reactions. The idea is to collect their insights, suggestions, and pain points to improve the product if possible.

Taking that feedback, you're going to iterate and refine you MVP. Address any shortcomings, usability issues, or areas of improvement that were identified by these early testers. This is a continuous process of you enhancing your product to align better with your customer's needs and expectations.

During the testing phase you want to define key metrics that align with your business objectives and track them. These metrics could include user engagement, conversion rates, customer satisfaction, or any other relevant performance indicators that pertain to your business. Analyzing these metrics helps you assess the effectiveness of the MVP and make data-driven decisions accordingly.

Here's the benefit on an MVP: based on the feedback, metrics, and insights gathered from this testing you can make an informed decision to either pivot your idea or proceed with further development. You should pivot if the testing showed significant flaws or gaps and proceed if the feedback is positive and validates the market demand.

These MVP testing phases allows you to fully understand whether your idea will fit into the market demand and make you money. It can validate your business idea, gather valuable feedback, and give you the opportunity to make informed decisions for committing significant resources. This reduces risks, maximizes learning, and empowers you as an entrepreneur to build products that truly meet customer needs and expectations.

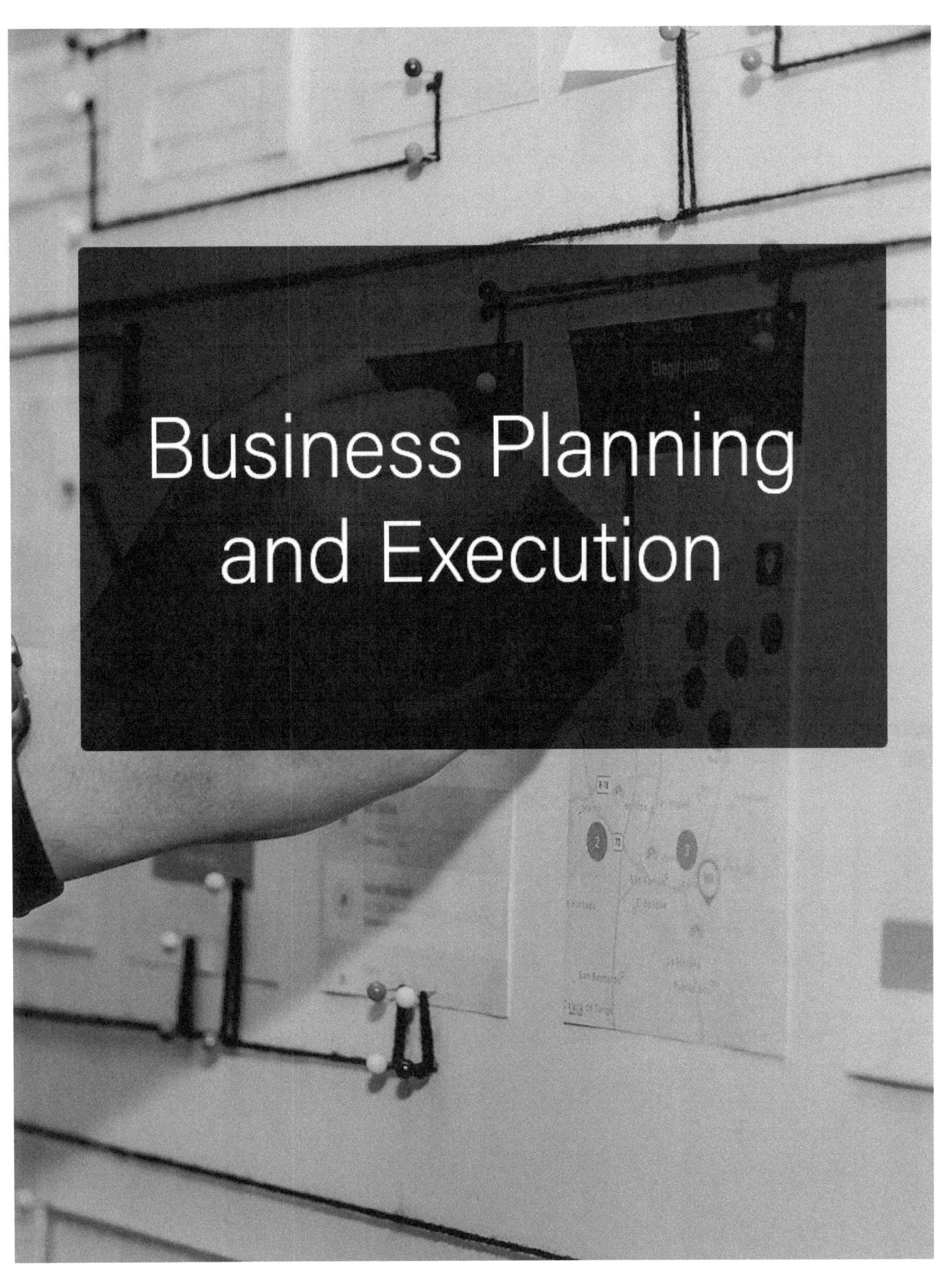

Business Planning
and Execution

Chapter 5: Business Planning and Execution

Next comes your well-crafted business plan with clear goals. They provide a roadmap not only for your decision-making, but guide your resource allocation, and ensure that your overall vision aligns with all other aspects of the business.

Writing a business plan and setting goals

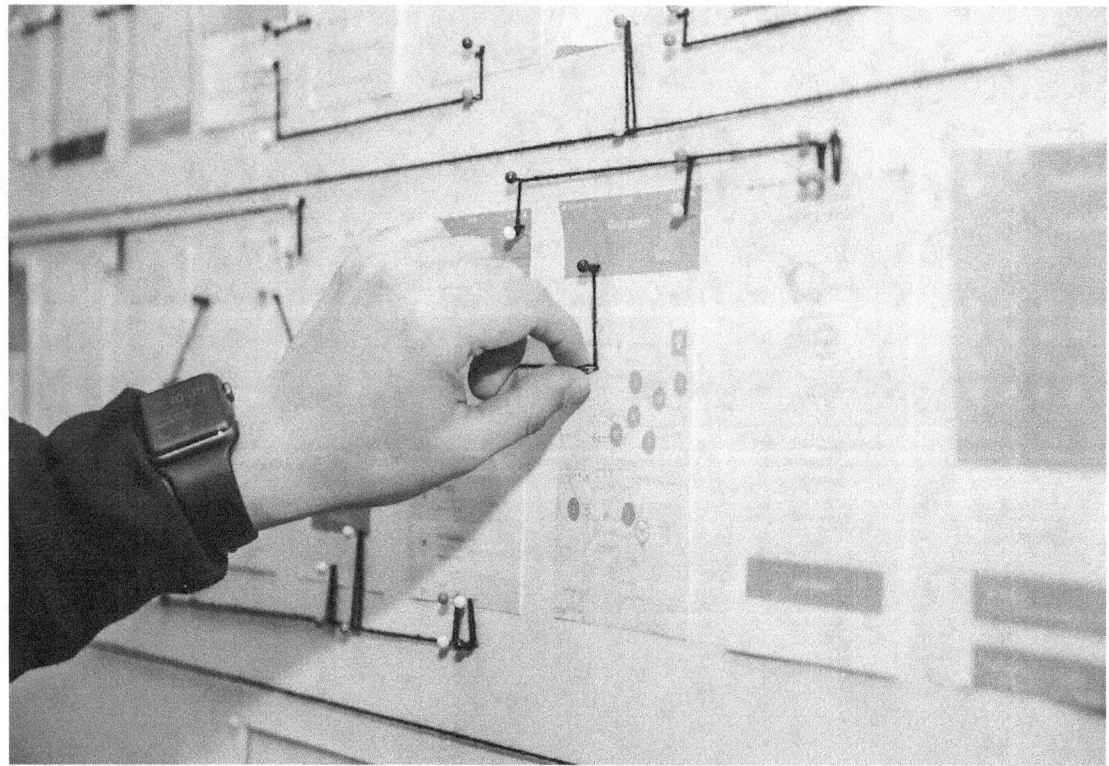

Your business plan needs to outline your vision, mission, target market, value proposition, competitive analysis, marketing strategies, operational plans, and financial projections. Include a description of your products or services, pricing strategy, distribution channels, and organizational structure. A well-written business plan serves as your blueprint not only for your business's future but also is necessary for attracting investors and securing funding.

You want to set SMART goals: Specific, Measurable, Achievable, Relevant, and Time-Bound goals that align with your business plan. Break down your long-term objectives into more short-term milestones to create a clear road map for yourself. While creating these goals, define key performance indicators (KPIs) that will help you measure progress and your successes.

When moving on to trying to reach your goals you can help yourself by breaking those goals down into smaller pieces. Identify the critical activities and/or resources that would be required to reach each goal. Then further prioritize these activities based on their impact so you can allocate resources, including finances, human capital, and technology effectively.

Effective execution requires a combination of strategic planning, flexibility, adaptability, and effective teamwork to turn your entrepreneurial aspirations into reality.

Building a team and delegating responsibilities

In order to scale your business and focus on strategic priorities it's important to build a strong team at your side.

Clearly define the roles and skills required to achieve your business goals. It helps if you sit down and identify the core competencies, expertise, and experiences necessary for each role you'd like filled. This enables you to create a team with the right talent.

If you want the top talent for your business, you'll need to be rigorous in your recruitment strategy. There are many channels to utilize like job boards, professional networks, and referrals to find the potential candidates. Use applications and interviews to assess their qualifications, cultural fit, and alignment with the position but also your vision. Look specifically for individuals who would bring diverse perspectives and passion for your industry.

You want to create a work environment that encourages collaboration and open communication. If you foster a culture of trust, respect, and innovation you'll have team members that share ideas, seek feedback, and share the growth mindset that is so important to your journey.

Communication is on you as well. You'll need to make sure that each team member understands their responsibilities and performance expectations. Ensure that everyone understands their role in contributing to the business's success. Give them clarity on goals, deadlines, and deliverables. This lets your team take ownership of their tasks and align their efforts with the overall objectives you've set.

Use your new teams' abilities and individual strengths to delegate tasks and responsibilities. Assess the workload and distribute the needed tasks evenly, taking into account each team member's capacity. Empower them by providing the necessary resources, authority, and autonomy to complete their assigned responsibilities. You need to be at the top of your game too so make sure to have the team work together instead of taking it all on yourself.

A cohesive and empowered team enables you to focus on strategic initiatives, fosters innovation, and propels your business forward.

Scaling and growing a business

Scaling and growing your business is an exciting prospect but you need to make sure you do it right. This involves expanding operations, increasing revenue, and reaching into new markets.

You need a growth strategy. This will outline your objectives, target markets, and expansion plans. Brainstorm and identify those opportunities for organic growth, such as entering new geographical markets or diversifying your product/services offerings. Consider the potential for strategic partnerships, acquisitions, or even franchising as potential avenues for growth.

Before you try to scale your business, you need to streamline operations. Efficient operations are crucial. Streamline processes, automate tasks where possible, and invest in technology that improves your productivity and reduces costs. By continuously optimizing your operations you can accommodate increasing demand and ensure your scalability.

Scaling and growth also involve your team. Hiring and developing talented individuals will drive growth. Building a strong leadership team will help you manage and align your organization toward those growth objectives.

You'll want to continuously monitor those KPIs and metrics to track progress toward your growth goals. Regularly assess the effectiveness of your strategies and make data-driven adjustments as needed. Stay agile and adaptable with the market dynamics and the needs of your customers.

To identify a new target market, you'll want to conduct that market research again. You need to understand the new needs, preferences, and buying behavior to successfully scale to include the new market.

Build a strong brand, it's the best investment you can make. Your brand should resonate with your target audience. Develop a compelling value proposition, communicate your unique selling points, and consistently deliver exceptional customer experiences and your name will follow the market. Build brand awareness with effective marketing like social media, public relations, and customer engagement.

Marketing and Sales

Chapter 6: Marketing and Sales

Successful marketing and sales strategies are built on a deep understanding of your target audience and their needs. By gaining insights into their preferences, motivations, and pain points, entrepreneurs can tailor their offerings and develop effective communication strategies.

Understanding your target audience and customer needs

That thorough market research comes into play again here. Those insights you gained into your target audience. Analyze demographic data, psychographic characteristics, and buying behaviors. Understand your audiences' preferences, challenges, and aspirations. Use surveys, interviews, and focus groups to gather that qualitative and quantitative data. This research forms the foundation for effective marketing and sales strategies.

Create fictional profiles, or buyer personas, that include your demographic information, motivations, goals, pain points, and buying patterns. This exercise helps you humanize your audience and tailor your marketing messages to resonate with their specific needs and desires. For instance, a buyer persona created from the market research you conducted could be a male named Brian, age 37, who's married with 2 kids. He works full-time after earning his bachelor's degree in marketing but still falls into a lower income bracket. He's loves hiking and camping with his family and dabbles in financial planning. Brian uses YouTube the most but will also spend some time on Facebook to stay in touch with friends and family and Reddit as he's part of a mountain biking community.

These buyer personas make your target audience people instead of data. You can easily identify their needs, challenges, and pain points because you can connect with them on a more human level. What problems are they trying to solve? How can your products or services address these needs effectively? By understanding their pain points, you can position your offerings as solutions that provide value and alleviate their struggles.

Developing a brand and messaging strategy

Your brand and message are what differentiates you from your competitors. A well-defined brand identity and effective messaging help create brand awareness, build trust with customers, and communicate the unique value of your products or services.

To help create this strategy identify your brand's core values, mission, and vision if you haven't already. Understand what sets your business apart from competitors and identify the key attributes that define your brand's personality. This includes things like brand voice, tone, and visual elements like logos, colors, and fonts.

After you've worked on that market research into your target audience and the buyer personas, it's much easier to develop the brand and voice of your company. Your value proposition is important and won't function without this important information.

Your value proposition needs to communicate the unique benefits and value that your brand offers to customers. It needs to highlight how your products or services solve their problems, fulfill their needs, or enhance their lives. Your value proposition should be concise, memorable, and differentiate you from your competitors.

Crafting a compelling brand story that engages customers emotionally is also important. Share the journey behind your business, your mission, and the impact you'd like to create. Use storytelling techniques to create an authentic connection with your audience and differentiate your brand from others.

While you're going to market on multiple channels, your brand messaging and touchpoints should be consistent across the board. From your website and social media platforms to advertising campaigns and customer interactions, maintain a consistent tone, voice, and visual identity. This helps establish brand recognition and builds trust among your audience.

The goal is to build relationships with your customers through personalized and meaningful interactions. Nurture brand loyalty by providing exceptional customer experiences and consistently delivering on your brand promise. Encourage all that customer feedback and address their needs to strengthen their connection to your brand.

As your business grows and the market changes, your brand and messaging strategy may also need to change. Monitor market trends, listen to customer feedback, and stay ahead of your competitors. Continuously evaluate and adapt your messaging to align with changing customer needs and preferences.

Building and executing a sales plan

If you want to drive revenue, acquire customers, and achieve sales targets then you need a well-defined sales plan. This outlines the strategies, tactics, and actions required to effectively sell products or services.

Start by setting clear and measurable sales goals and objectives. Define your revenue targets, customer acquisition goals, and other key KPIs that align with those overall business objections you determined earlier. This provides a nice, clear direction for your sales efforts.

Develop strategies and tactics to now achieve your sales goals. You'll need to determine the most effective sales channels and approaches based on your target audience, market research, and those buyer profiles. This may include direct sales, online sales, partnerships, referrals, or other distribution methods. Create a comprehensive sales playbook that outlines the steps, processes, and techniques for your sales team to follow.

You may need to build a skilled and motivated sales team for this. Hire individuals who align with your company culture and possess strong communication and relationship-building skills. These are the people that will be communicating directly with your customers.

Effective sales processes lead to continued success. Streamlining your sales cycle helps and also enables efficient sales execution. Think about using customer relationship management (CRM) software to track leads, manage customer interactions, and monitor sales activities. You can even implement sales automation tools to enhance productivity and streamline administrative tasks.

A well-executed sales plan requires continuous evaluation, adaptation, and a customer-centric approach to effectively meet market demands and drive sales success.

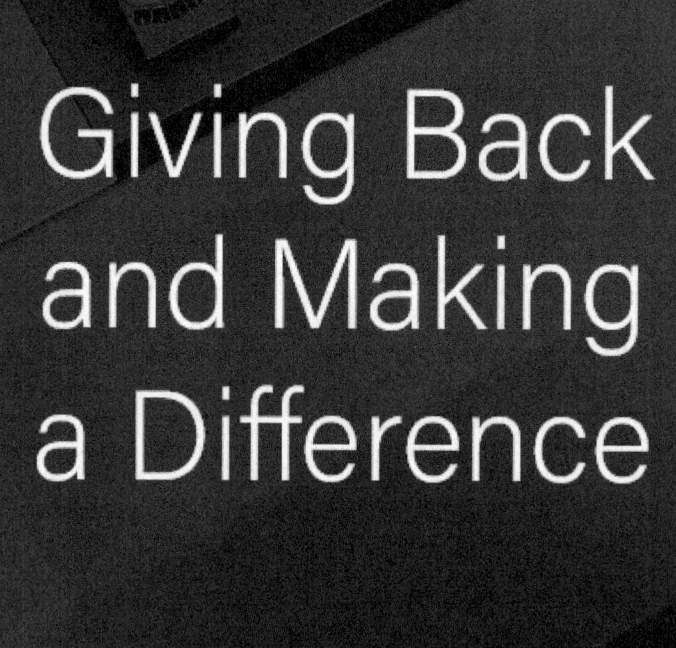
Giving Back
and Making
a Difference

Chapter 7: Giving Back and Making a Difference

Using business as a way to make a difference goes beyond profitability and success. It involves making a positive impact on society and the environment. By incorporating social and environmental responsibility into their business practices, entrepreneurs have the opportunity to give back and make a difference.

Using business as a force for good

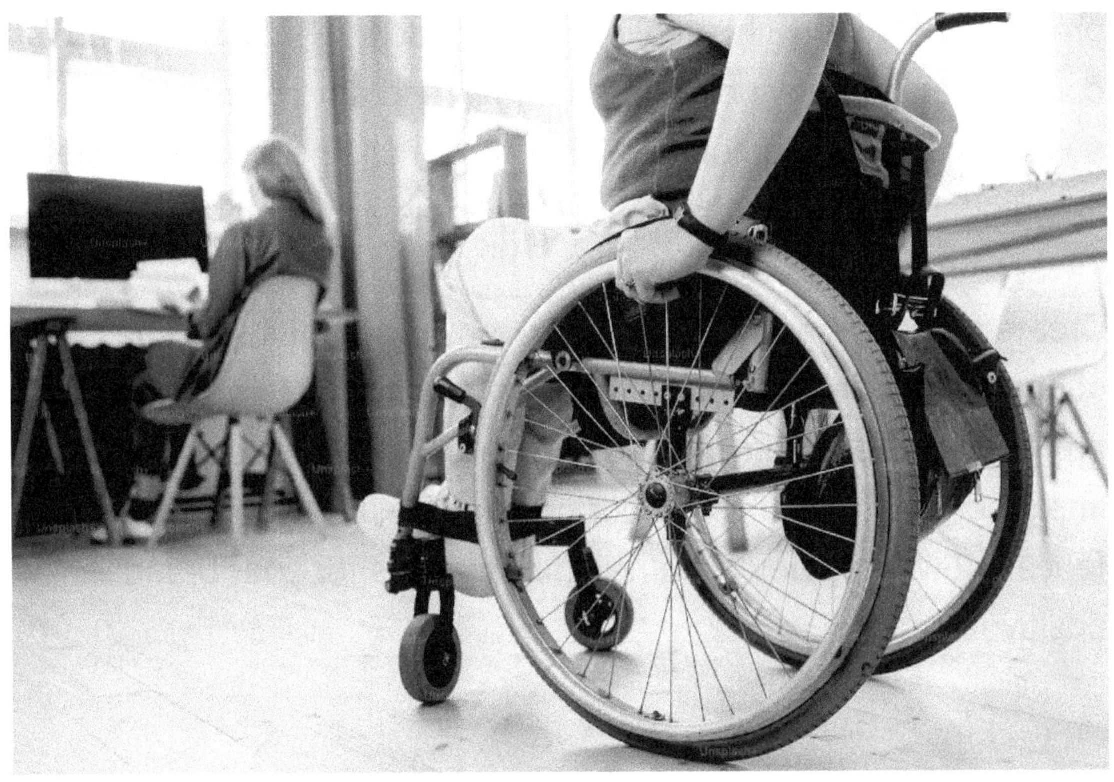

Once you've defined those business purposes and core values you can identify social and environmental issues that resonate with your values and align with your industry. This will guide your efforts in giving back and making a meaningful impact.

Adopting sustainable business practices can minimize your environmental footprint. This can include reducing waste, conserving energy, using eco-friendly materials, and implementing recycling programs. By prioritizing sustainability, you contribute to a healthier planet and inspire others to do the same.

Ensure your supply chain adheres to ethical and responsible practices. Partner with suppliers and vendors who share your commitment to fair labor, human rights, and environmental sustainability. By promoting ethical supply chains, you contribute to a global ecosystem that respects people and the planet.

Create a positive and inclusive work environment that values and supports your employees. Offer opportunities for personal and professional development, promote the work-life balance, and implement fair and ethical labor practices. When your employees feel empowered, they become ambassadors for your brand's positive impact.

Incorporating social responsibility into business strategy

Develop a comprehensive Corporate Social Responsibility (CSR) strategy that aligns with your values and addresses social issues. This can involve supporting local communities, donating a portion of profits to charitable causes, or volunteering your time and resources. Collaborate with nonprofit organizations or create your own initiatives to make a positive impact.

Set goals for your social responsibility initiatives. Define the desired outcomes and the specific actions you will take to achieve them. These can be incorporated into your day-to-day operations. This includes considering ethical sourcing and supply chain practices, minimizing waste and environmental impact, promoting diversity and inclusion within your workforce, and prioritizing fair and responsible labor practices. Integrate these principles into your policies, procedures, and decision-making processes.

Make sure to engage your stakeholders, including employees, customers, suppliers, and local community, in your social responsibility efforts, Communicate your goals, initiatives, and progress transparently. Encourage feedback and collaboration to ensure that your actions align with the expectations and needs of all your stakeholders.

Building a legacy beyond financial success

While financial success is often a primary goal, building a lasting legacy goes beyond monetary achievements. It involves making a meaningful and lasting impact on the world and leaving a positive imprint on people's lives. A legacy encompasses the values, principles, and contributions that endure long after the business journey ends.

Start by defining your purpose and values and what truly matters to you beyond financial gains. Identify the principles and beliefs that guide your actions and decision-making. This clarity will shape the legacy you aspire to create.

Fostering positive relationships goes a long way. Invest in building strong relationships with stakeholders, including employees, customers, partners, and the community. Foster a culture of trust, respect, and collaboration. Leave a lasting impression through your integrity, empathy, and genuine care for others.

You can take the time to mentor others and inspire other new entrepreneurs or individuals in the same industry as you. Share your knowledge, experiences, and lessons learned. Encourage and empower others to pursue their dreams and make a difference in their own lives and communities.

Along those lines, create a culture of continuous learning and growth within your organization. Encourage your employees to develop their skills, pursue their passions, and reach their full potential. Invest in their professional and personal development. By nurturing a learning environment, you leave a legacy of empowered and fulfilled individuals.

Think about documenting your entrepreneurial journey and share your story. Capture the challenges, triumphs, and lessons learned along the way. Share your insights through books, articles, speaking engagements, or digital platforms. Inspire others with your experiences and provide a road map for them to follow.

Your legacy is the imprint you leave on people's lives and the positive change you bring to the world.

Entrepreneurial Mindset for Life

Chapter 8: Entrepreneurial Mindset for Life

The entrepreneurial mindset is not limited to business ventures alone; it is a powerful approach that can be applied to all aspects of life. By embracing the entrepreneurial mindset, individuals can foster personal and professional growth, seize opportunities, and overcome challenges.

Applying the entrepreneurial mindset to personal and professional growth

By adopting this mindset, you can navigate challenges, embrace opportunities, and continuously evolve in all aspects of life. The growth mindset encourages you to embrace the belief that abilities and skills can be cultivated through dedication and effort. It allows you to view challenges as opportunities for learning and improvement not only in business but in life in general. By maintaining a growth mindset, you remain open to new experiences and are constantly seeking self-improvement.

Setting clear goals, SMART goals, works in your personal life. Breaking down your goals into specific, measurable, achievable, relevant, and time-bound categories teaches you how to approach any problem or situation. The focused approach propels you towards growth and accomplishment.

The entrepreneurial mindset teaches you to step outside your comfort zone. You tackle new adventures because you've learned that the fear of failure holds you back. Now, you can see failures as a path for growth and new opportunities. Taking risks helps you discover new paths to take, expands your horizons, and helps to unlock your potential.

Resilience and adaptability are equally valuable. Cultivate resilience and find the ability to bounce back from any setback, learn from your failures, and stay committed to your goals no matter what. Being adaptable means that you'll thrive in the ever-changing world we live in, and you'll be ready and able to seize new opportunities that come your way.

Entrepreneurs learn to thrive on creativity and innovation. Foster creativity by seeking new perspectives, exploring diverse interests, and embracing a spirit of curiosity. Innovate by finding unique solutions to challenges and constantly seeking improvement in life.

Developing a lifelong learning strategy

Lifelong learning is the key to personal and professional growth, enabling you to adapt to a rapidly changing world and stay ahead in your field and life. To cultivate a lifelong learning mindset, it's essential to develop a strategic approach that maximizes the benefits of continuous learning.

Clarify your learning objectives. You need to identify the knowledge, skills, and expertise that you wish to gain or enhance. Consider both your personal and professional lives when making this list. Setting specific learning goals provides not only direction but motivation for your lifelong learning journey.

Figure out what learning resources are available to reach those goals. This could include books, online courses, workshops, conferences, webinars, podcasts, or even mentoring programs.

You'll want to explore a combination of both formal and informal learning opportunities to expand your knowledge base.

Try to commit to a regular learning schedule. Allocate a dedicated time each week or month for learning activities. Treat this as a non-negotiable part of your routine. Consistency is key when it comes to building momentum and making continuous learning a habit.

Take time to reflect on your learning journey. Assess your progress, strengths, and areas for improvement. Self-reflection helps you track your growth and identify areas where you need further development. Use assessments, feedback from mentors, or self-evaluation tools to help you gain insights into your learning effectiveness.

It helps to surround yourself with like-minded people who are on lifelong learning journeys themselves. Try to find forums to engage with or social media groups. There may even be some local meetups related to your areas of interest. Collaborate, share ideas, and learn from others' experiences. Networking within your field can also open doors to new learning opportunities and even mentorships.

It's important to take the chance to apply your newfound knowledge and skills in practical settings. Seek out opportunities to use them through projects, volunteering, or even professional engagements. Sharing your knowledge with others, such as through teaching or mentoring, solidifies your own understanding and contributes back to the learning community.

Stay curious. This isn't a destination but rather a continuous process. Be adaptable and willing to adjust your learning goals as needed to stay relevant in a changing world.

Navigating career transitions and new opportunities

Career transitions and new opportunities can be a combination of exciting and a challenge. Whether you're changing industries, pursuing a promotion, or exploring a completely different path, navigating these transitions requires careful planning and adaptability.

Start by reflecting on your skills, strengths, passions, and values. You're going to want to assess how they align with your desired career transition or new opportunity. Make sure to think on your own motivations and what you hope to achieve with this change. This type of self-assessment provides a solid foundation for making informed decisions and setting realistic goals.

It can help to thoroughly research the industry, role, or opportunity that you're considering. Look into the job market trends, the required skills, and the potential challenges you'll face. Speaking with other professionals in the field can help you gain insights and get sound advice. You may want to look into getting some experience through internships, part-time work, or volunteering first to see if it's the right path for you. The more you learn, the better equipped you are to make informed decisions.

If you've already chosen a career transition, then think about identifying the potential gaps in your skillset. Taking proactive steps to bridge these gaps through courses, certifications, or workshops can ease the change into something highly enjoyable instead of stressful.

When it comes to your personal skills, highlight those for yourself that will transfer from your previous position to the new opportunity. Emphasize how these skills can add value in the new context. This is a great way to combat the imposter syndrome that can accompany a job change.

Finding professional mentors is never a bad idea. Their insights and advice can help you navigate potential obstacles and provide valuable support. Seek out individuals who have successfully made similar transitions to the one you're planning. Their firsthand experiences can be invaluable as you navigate your own path.

Your entrepreneurial mindset will set you up with the resilience and persistence to tackle any opportunity that comes your way, especially if you're already embracing that lifelong learning concept.

Each transition brings valuable opportunities for growth, learning, and personal fulfillment.

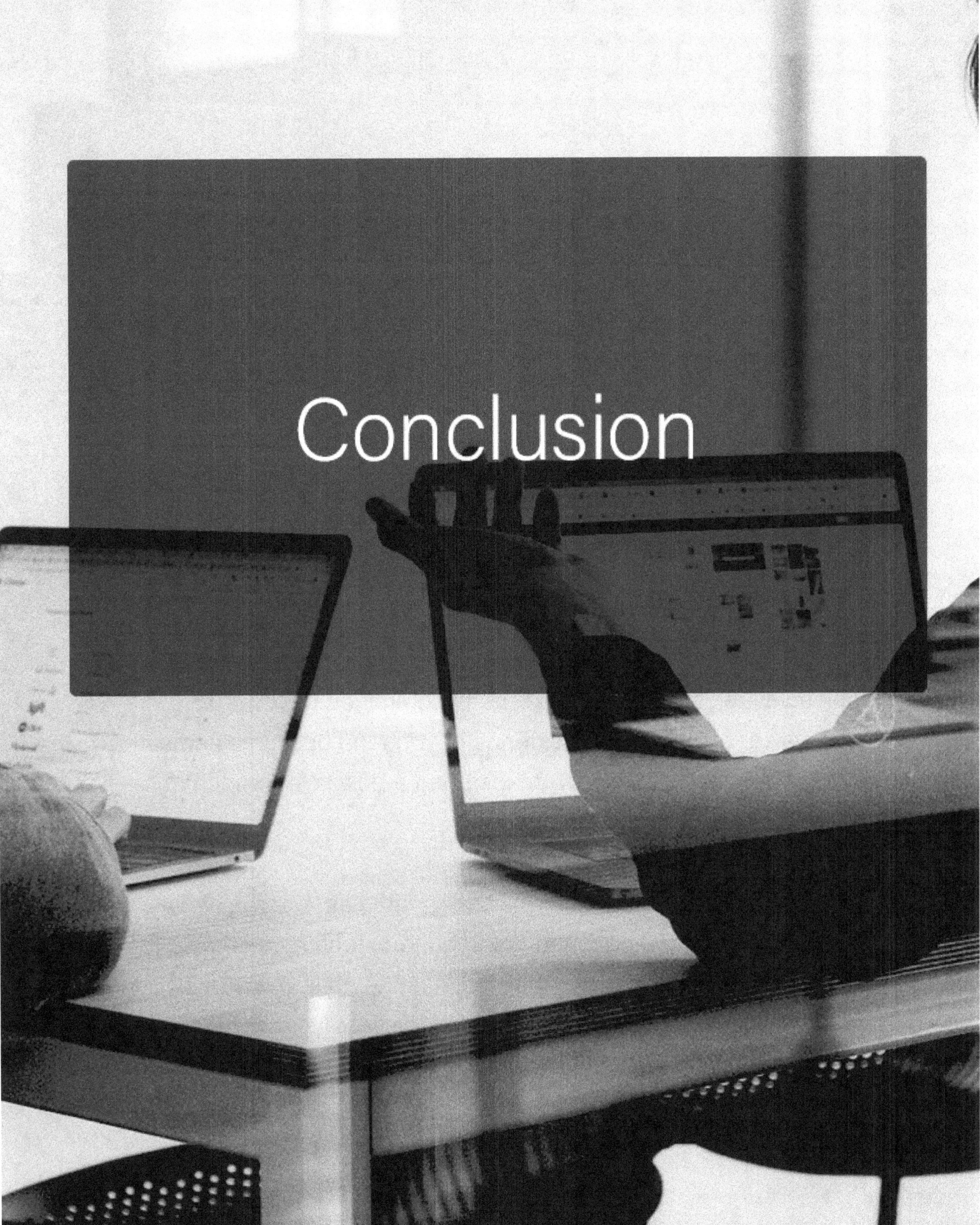
Conclusion

Conclusion

On the journey of entrepreneurship, success hinges on a combination of mindset and strategies. Throughout this book, we have explored various aspects essential to entrepreneurial success, from developing the right mindset to executing effective strategies. By bringing it all together, you can position yourself for growth, adapt to challenges, and seize opportunities with confidence.

Bringing it all together:

The entrepreneurial mindset serves as the foundation for success. It encompasses traits such as resilience, adaptability, and growth. By cultivating these qualities, you can navigate obstacles, embrace risk, and remain committed to your goals. The power of this mindset extends beyond the business and can be applied to personal growth, fostering a holistic approach to lifelong development.

To effectively implement this mindset strategies, play a pivotal role. From idea generation to market understanding, planning to execution, each step is crucial. You must be able to validate your ideas, understand market demand, and assess your competition to carve out your unique position. Building a strong team and delegating responsibilities enables you to leverage all the diverse skills and expertise, fostering that important growth and scalability.

Marketing and sales strategies are vital for connecting to your target audience and addressing the needs of your customers. Developing your brand, crafting compelling messaging, and executing a sales plan are integral components of a successful business. Incorporating social responsibility into these plans and giving back not only fulfills a greater purpose but also strengthens your brand loyalty and community engagement.

Overcoming failure and handling success are critical aspects of this journey. Learning from your failures fuels that success you're looking for by providing valuable lessons and insights. Likewise, managing success requires you to avoid the drag of complacency and encourages you to continuously push boundaries. Finding a balance between humility and confidence fosters growth and ensures a sustained progress.

You need to be able to stay agile and adapt to changing circumstances. Navigating career transitions and exploring new opportunities demand self-reflection, skill development, and networking. Lifelong learning, coupled with the growth mindset, empowers individuals to thrive in an ever-evolving world.

Success as an entrepreneur relies on this multifaceted approach that combines the right mindset and effective strategies. By developing this entrepreneurial mindset, you can overcome all life's challenges, embrace those risks that will come around, and continuously grow both personally and professionally. Applying this mindset to all aspects of life fosters a holistic approach to growth and in turn fulfillment.

The entrepreneurial journey is a dynamic and transformative process. It requires an unwavering commitment to personal development, a willingness to take calculated risks, and a mindset that embraces challenges and growth. By integrating the principles discussed here, you can embark on a fulfilling journey of entrepreneurship, equipped with the mindset and strategies necessary for lasting success and a meaningful impact on your life and the world around you.